PRINCEWILL LAGANG

The Evolution of Love: Historical and Psychological Perspectives

Copyright © 2023 by Princewill Lagang

All rights reserved. No part of this publication may be reproduced, stored or transmitted in any form or by any means, electronic, mechanical, photocopying, recording, scanning, or otherwise without written permission from the publisher. It is illegal to copy this book, post it to a website, or distribute it by any other means without permission.

Princewill Lagang asserts the moral right to be identified as the author of this work.

First edition

This book was professionally typeset on Reedsy.
Find out more at reedsy.com

Contents

Introduction	1
Love in Ancient Cultures	3
The Influence of Literature and Mythology	5
Love in Different Historical Periods	8
The Emergence of Romantic Love	11
Love and Psychology	14
Cultural Variations in Love	17
The Modern Notion of Love	20
Love's Role in Relationships	23
Love and Gender Dynamics	26
The Science of Lasting Love	29
Reflection and Future Perspectives	32

Introduction

Love, as a concept, has captivated the human imagination for centuries. It is a force that transcends time, culture, and geography, touching the very core of our being. In "The Evolution of Love: Historical and Psychological Perspectives," we embark on a journey to explore the multifaceted nature of love, examining it through the lenses of both history and psychology. By delving into the past and understanding the intricate workings of the human mind, we aim to uncover the fascinating story of how love has evolved over time.

In this opening chapter, we lay the groundwork for our exploration by introducing the central theme of the book: the interplay between historical shifts and psychological insights that have shaped our understanding of love. Love's journey is one that has unfolded over millennia, leaving its mark on ancient civilizations, literature, art, and personal narratives. From the passionate tales of gods and mortals in ancient mythologies to the tender expressions of affection in historical texts, love has been a constant companion on the human voyage.

As we embark on this journey, we acknowledge the significance of understanding how love has transformed over time. By comprehending the historical contexts in which love was conceptualized and expressed, we can gain a deeper appreciation for the forces that have shaped our current perceptions of relationships, emotions, and human connections. Simultaneously, delving into the psychological dimensions of love allows us to grasp the intricate mechanics of attraction, attachment, and intimacy that make love such a potent and complex force.

Throughout this book, we will explore how various cultural, social, and economic factors have influenced the perception and experience of love. We will analyze the emergence of romantic love as a distinct concept, unravel the threads of attachment theory and cognitive processes that underlie our emotional bonds, and investigate how love has been portrayed and practiced across diverse cultures. We will also consider the changing landscape of love in the modern world, shaped by technology, globalization, and shifting societal norms.

But this book is not just a historical and psychological exploration; it is an invitation to reflect upon our own lives and relationships. As we journey through the chapters ahead, we encourage you, the reader, to engage with the material and ponder the ways in which the evolution of love has left its mark on your own experiences. By connecting the past and the present, the historical and the psychological, we hope to offer a comprehensive and enlightening view of love—a view that acknowledges its complexities and celebrates its enduring presence in the human story.

In the pages that follow, we invite you to join us on a voyage through time and human emotion, as we uncover the layers of meaning behind one of life's most profound and captivating phenomena: love.

Love in Ancient Cultures

Love, in its various forms, has been a cornerstone of human experience since time immemorial. As we journey back through the annals of history, we find that the concept of love has held a significant place within the tapestry of ancient civilizations and cultures. In this chapter, we delve into the rich and diverse portrayals of love in these ancient societies, seeking to uncover the origins of our modern understanding of this complex emotion.

Love's Many Facets in Ancient Civilizations:

In the ancient world, love was depicted in a multitude of ways, each reflective of the cultural, societal, and spiritual values of the time. From the passionate and tempestuous affairs of Greek mythology to the harmonious and duty-bound relationships of ancient China, love took on various hues, serving as a mirror to the cultural norms and expectations of these societies. We explore the symbolic roles of love in religious rituals, familial bonds, and social hierarchies, revealing how love was both a deeply personal experience and a communal force that bound individuals and communities together.

The Historical Footprint of Ancient Love:

As we examine love's portrayal in ancient texts, artwork, and stories, we uncover the roots of many modern perceptions of love. The notions of romantic yearning, unrequited love, and the sacrifices made in the name of affection can be traced back to the narratives of ancient civilizations. The epic tales of heroism, tragedy, and divine interventions that were spun in these early cultures have shaped our collective understanding of love's complexity and transformative power.

The Influence on Modern Perceptions:

The ways in which love was revered, expressed, and understood in ancient times have left an indelible mark on how we conceptualize love today. The echoes of ancient ideals of devotion, loyalty, and passion reverberate in our contemporary relationships, literature, and popular culture. By studying how love was intertwined with the fabric of daily life in ancient societies, we gain insights into the roots of our own yearnings, insecurities, and desires.

In examining love through the lens of ancient cultures, we gain a deeper appreciation for the historical perspectives that continue to shape our present understanding. As we traverse the stories of gods and mortals, kings and peasants, lovers and companions, we come to recognize that the foundations of love's allure remain timeless, even as they adapt to the changing tides of history.

In the chapters that follow, we will journey through different historical periods, exploring how love has transformed in response to the ever-shifting sands of time. By understanding where we've come from, we are better equipped to navigate the landscapes of love in our own lives, relationships, and societies.

The Influence of Literature and Mythology

In the vast realm of human creativity, few forces have been as instrumental in shaping our understanding of love as literature, mythology, and religious texts. These narratives, often laden with symbolism and emotional resonance, have the power to transcend time, leaving an indelible mark on societal perspectives of love. In this chapter, we delve into the intricate interplay between stories and love, exploring how these narratives have sculpted our collective consciousness and influenced the way we perceive and experience this complex emotion.

The Luminous Tapestry of Love in Narratives:
Throughout history, writers, poets, and storytellers have woven intricate tales that bring love to life in its myriad forms. From the epic poetry of ancient civilizations to the timeless novels of modernity, these stories have captured the essence of love's joys and tribulations. The passionate declarations of love, the heart-wrenching tragedies of unrequited affection, and the enduring bonds of companionship—all find their expression within the pages of literature.

Mythology's Impact on Love Perceptions:
Myths, with their gods, goddesses, and heroic figures, have been instrumental in shaping cultural perceptions of love. These stories often explore the boundaries between mortals and the divine, portraying love as a force

capable of transcending the human realm. The tales of forbidden love, divine interventions, and sacrifices made for the sake of affection have left an enduring imprint on the way we understand the power and complexities of love.

Religious Texts as Guides to Love:
Across cultures and faiths, religious texts have offered insights into the spiritual dimensions of love. They often emphasize the virtues of compassion, empathy, and selflessness, portraying love as a divine mandate. Whether through parables, teachings, or sacred stories, these texts have not only guided individual relationships but also shaped broader societal values related to love and human interactions.

The Evolution of Cultural Norms through Narratives:
Literature and mythology are more than just entertainment; they serve as mirrors reflecting the cultural norms and values of their times. By studying how love was depicted in various eras, we gain insights into the shifting sands of societal expectations, gender dynamics, and familial roles. These narratives have both perpetuated and challenged conventional notions of love, contributing to the evolution of our understanding.

The Modern Echoes of Ancient Narratives:
The stories of love that have survived the passage of time continue to resonate in our modern world. The archetypes of star-crossed lovers, heroic quests for affection, and the enduring power of love's transformative journey are woven into the fabric of contemporary literature, film, and art. By recognizing these echoes, we acknowledge the enduring influence of the narratives that have shaped our perceptions.

In exploring the profound impact of literature, mythology, and religious texts on our understanding of love, we uncover a rich tapestry of emotions, ideals, and cultural shifts. These narratives not only reflect the complexities of human connection but also offer insights into the deepest corners of our hearts and minds. As we move forward in this exploration of love's evolution, we will continue to trace the threads of storytelling that have woven together our collective experiences of this timeless emotion.

Love in Different Historical Periods

As time marches forward, the concept of love weaves its way through the ever-changing tapestry of human history. The expression, understanding, and even prioritization of love have evolved across eras, shaped by the unique interplay of cultural, social, and economic forces. In this chapter, we embark on a chronological journey through various historical periods, tracing the evolution of love and uncovering the myriad ways in which it has been perceived, experienced, and valued.

Ancient Love:
   In ancient civilizations, love often found itself intertwined with societal duties and expectations. Marriages were often arranged for strategic reasons, and familial alliances were prioritized over individual desires. Yet, within these structures, expressions of love still emerged, showcasing the resilience of the human heart. We explore how love was perceived in societies where familial bonds and communal well-being often took precedence over personal affections.

Medieval Notions of Chivalry and Courtly Love:
   The medieval period brought forth the romantic ideals of chivalry and courtly love. These concepts placed love on a pedestal, often exalting the admiration of a beloved figure from a distance. The troubadours of the time composed poems and songs extolling the virtues of devotion and reverence, shaping the romantic ideals that would continue to influence love narratives

for centuries.

Renaissance and Enlightenment Shifts:

The Renaissance era saw a resurgence of interest in individuality, aesthetics, and the human experience. This shift also extended to love, as notions of personal affection and emotional intimacy gained prominence. Philosophers and writers of the Enlightenment further explored the rational and emotional aspects of love, heralding a new era of exploration into the complexities of human connection.

Victorian Virtues and Social Norms:

The Victorian era was characterized by a complex interplay of strict social norms and repressed desires. Love often existed within the boundaries set by societal expectations, and courtship rituals were codified. However, beneath the surface, there were undercurrents of yearning and hidden emotions that found expression through art and literature.

Modern Times and Changing Landscapes:

The 20th and 21st centuries have witnessed significant shifts in societal norms and values, impacting how love is understood and experienced. Rapid urbanization, globalization, and changing gender dynamics have reshaped the landscape of love. The emergence of romantic love as a dominant cultural narrative, along with the exploration of diverse relationship models, highlights the ongoing evolution of love in modern times.

Cultural, Social, and Economic Influences:

Throughout history, cultural, social, and economic factors have exerted their influence on love's expressions and meanings. From economic considerations affecting marriage choices to cultural norms shaping gender roles, these factors have both constrained and enabled the experience of love. We examine how love has been shaped by wars, revolutions, economic booms, and societal upheavals, reflecting the broader currents of human existence.

By exploring love across these different historical epochs, we gain a panoramic view of how love has transformed and adapted over time. Each era's unique blend of values, beliefs, and circumstances has left an indelible mark on our understanding of this intricate emotion. As we navigate through history, we recognize that love is not a static concept but rather a dynamic force that continues to evolve, reflecting the ever-changing world in which it resides.

The Emergence of Romantic Love

In the intricate tapestry of human emotions, one thread stands out prominently: romantic love. Unlike the familial and communal bonds of the past, romantic love emerged as a distinct and powerful force that would come to shape the way we view and experience relationships. In this chapter, we delve into the origins and evolution of romantic love, tracing its emergence as a dominant cultural narrative and exploring the cultural and literary movements that played a pivotal role in its ascent.

From Duty to Desire:

The historical transition from arranged marriages and strategic alliances to marriages based on personal choice and affection marked a significant shift in the perception of love. The emergence of romantic love was characterized by a focus on personal emotions, individual desires, and mutual affection. Love was no longer solely a societal obligation; it became an intimate and deeply personal experience.

Literature's Role in Shaping Romantic Ideals:

The world of literature, particularly during the Romantic era, played a profound role in shaping the ideals and narratives of romantic love. Poets and writers celebrated the intensity of emotional connections, often elevating love to a transcendental experience. The works of figures like Lord Byron, Jane Austen, and Emily Dickinson helped solidify the romantic ideals that continue to resonate with us today.

Cultural Movements and Romanticism:

The Romantic movement of the 18th and 19th centuries was a reaction against the rationalism and industrialization of the time. It emphasized emotion, nature, and individuality—all of which found resonance in the burgeoning concept of romantic love. The celebration of intense feelings, passionate yearnings, and the sublime beauty of emotions aligned with the growing cultural importance of love in human relationships.

Social Changes and the Embrace of Sentiment:

As societal norms shifted and notions of individualism gained traction, the space for romantic love expanded. The rise of the middle class, along with increased leisure time, allowed for greater emotional exploration. The sentimentalism of the Victorian era, expressed through poetry, novels, and visual art, heightened the focus on emotional depth and personal connection.

Media's Influence on Romantic Narratives:

With the advent of mass media, romantic narratives gained further traction and permeated popular culture. Films, television shows, and popular music reinforced the ideals of romantic love, shaping how it was perceived by a wider audience. The stories of star-crossed lovers, dramatic gestures of affection, and the pursuit of one's "soulmate" became embedded in the collective consciousness.

Love as a Core Cultural Narrative:

The emergence of romantic love as a central cultural narrative reflects a broader societal shift towards prioritizing emotional fulfillment and personal happiness. This narrative not only influenced how individuals approached relationships but also impacted societal values, norms, and expectations related to love and marriage.

The emergence of romantic love marked a transformation in the human experience of emotion and connection. As we continue to navigate the complex terrain of relationships and emotions, it is essential to understand how this concept developed, and how cultural and artistic movements played a role in shaping our understanding of romantic love. By tracing the trajectory of this profound shift, we gain insight into the intricate dance between the human heart, societal change, and the power of artistic expression.

Love and Psychology

The realm of human emotions and relationships has long fascinated psychologists, who seek to unravel the intricate threads that bind us together. Love, with its complex interplay of emotions, attachments, and desires, has been a subject of keen psychological inquiry. In this chapter, we delve into the psychological dimensions of love, exploring the theories, studies, and insights that shed light on the inner workings of this powerful and enigmatic emotion.

Psychological Theories of Love:

Psychologists have proposed various theories to explain the nature of love and its different facets. From Sternberg's Triangular Theory of Love, which breaks down love into intimacy, passion, and commitment, to Maslow's Hierarchy of Needs, which places love as a fundamental human need, these theories offer frameworks for understanding the multifaceted nature of love.

Attachment Styles and Love:

Attachment theory has played a crucial role in understanding how our early experiences shape our patterns of love and relationships. The attachment styles—secure, anxious, and avoidant—provide insights into how individuals approach intimacy, seek emotional connection, and respond to separations or conflicts. These attachment styles influence the way we form and maintain romantic bonds.

Emotions and Love:

Emotions form the bedrock of human experience, and they are inextricably linked with the concept of love. Joy, affection, desire, jealousy, and even pain are emotions that weave through the tapestry of romantic relationships. Psychologists delve into the intricate web of emotional experiences associated with love, examining how they can both nurture and challenge the connections we forge.

Cognitive Processes in Love:
Love often involves a complex interplay of thoughts, perceptions, and cognitive processes. Cognitive psychology examines how our thoughts and interpretations of events influence our emotions and behaviors in relationships. Cognitive biases, such as idealization or negative distortions, can impact how we perceive our partners and experiences of love.

The Role of Neurobiology:
Advances in neuroscience have deepened our understanding of love by revealing the neural mechanisms at play. Neuroimaging studies have shown that areas of the brain associated with reward, attachment, and empathy are activated when we experience feelings of love. These insights provide a physiological basis for our emotional experiences.

Love's Evolution and Challenges:
Psychological research underscores that love is not a static emotion but a dynamic process that evolves over time. Long-term relationships undergo changes, from the initial infatuation to deeper emotional bonds. Understanding the challenges that arise—such as conflict resolution, communication, and maintaining intimacy—can guide individuals in navigating the complexities of love.

The field of psychology offers a rich landscape for exploring the inner workings of love, drawing on theories, studies, and scientific insights. By unraveling the psychological dimensions of love, we gain a deeper appreciation for the profound impact that emotions, attachment styles, and cognitive processes have on our relationships and personal well-being. As we move forward, we continue to navigate the intricate terrain of love, armed with psychological insights that illuminate the path ahead.

Cultural Variations in Love

Love, a universal emotion, is woven into the fabric of human experience across the globe. Yet, the ways in which love is perceived, expressed, and valued can vary greatly from culture to culture. In this chapter, we embark on a journey through diverse cultural landscapes, exploring the nuanced ways in which different societies understand and manifest the complex emotion of love. By examining cultural norms, values, and practices, we gain insights into the rich tapestry of human connections across the world.

Cultural Definitions of Love:
Cultures around the world hold unique definitions of love, each shaped by historical, societal, and spiritual factors. Some cultures prioritize familial bonds and communal well-being, while others place a strong emphasis on romantic love and personal emotions. By examining these variations, we uncover the diverse ways love is woven into the narratives of different societies.

Expressions of Affection:
The outward expression of love varies greatly across cultures, ranging from reserved and subtle to overt and passionate. Cultural norms influence how affection is shown in public and private spaces. Gestures, verbal expressions, and physical contact—each influenced by cultural context—shape the ways in which love is communicated and understood.

Arranged Marriages and Love Matches:

The dichotomy between arranged marriages and love matches showcases the intricate relationship between culture, tradition, and love. In some cultures, arranged marriages emphasize compatibility, familial harmony, and long-term stability. In others, love matches based on personal choice and affection take center stage. Both approaches reflect differing cultural perspectives on the role of love in relationships.

Family and Community Influences:

In many cultures, the influence of family and community is deeply intertwined with the experience of love. Familial approval, elders' guidance, and societal expectations shape not only the individuals' choices but also the trajectory of their relationships. The interplay between individual desires and communal considerations illuminates the intricate balance cultures strike.

Spirituality and Love:

Religious and spiritual beliefs often play a significant role in shaping cultural attitudes towards love. From viewing love as a divine gift to embracing selflessness and compassion, cultural expressions of love are interwoven with spiritual teachings. Love's connection to broader moral and ethical frameworks deepens its significance in cultural contexts.

Changing Dynamics in a Globalized World:

As societies become increasingly interconnected through technology and globalization, cultural boundaries blur, leading to the exchange of ideas and practices. This interconnectedness brings both opportunities for cross-cultural understanding and challenges as traditional norms encounter new influences.

By examining cultural variations in love, we not only appreciate the diversity of human experience but also recognize the universal desire for connection and emotional fulfillment. Each culture's unique approach to love enriches our understanding of the intricate ways in which love shapes our lives. As we journey through different cultural perspectives, we gain a broader lens through which to view love's myriad manifestations and the depth of its impact on the human experience.

The Modern Notion of Love

In the rapidly changing landscape of the modern world, the concept of love has undergone significant transformations. Technology, globalization, and evolving social structures have given rise to new dynamics and perspectives on love. In this chapter, we delve into the modern notion of love, exploring how society perceives and prioritizes this complex emotion in the face of contemporary challenges and opportunities.

Love in the Digital Age:

The advent of technology has revolutionized the way we connect and communicate, influencing how love is experienced and expressed. Online dating, social media, and virtual interactions have opened up new avenues for forging connections, while also introducing challenges such as digital misunderstandings and the paradox of choice. We explore how technology has redefined the boundaries of intimacy and reshaped the dynamics of modern relationships.

Globalization's Impact on Love:

Globalization has bridged geographical divides, bringing people from diverse cultures and backgrounds into contact with one another. This intercultural exchange has enriched our understanding of love by exposing us to a broader spectrum of perspectives. Cross-cultural relationships, long-distance love, and the blending of traditions highlight the ways in which love transcends borders and nationalities.

Changing Social Structures and Values:

The shifting landscape of gender roles, marriage norms, and family structures has influenced how love is perceived and pursued. Changing expectations around work-life balance, individual aspirations, and partnership dynamics have reshaped the criteria for successful relationships. The modern notion of love embraces diversity and flexibility, accommodating a wider range of relationship models.

Prioritizing Self-Expression and Fulfillment:

Modern societies place a premium on individualism and personal fulfillment. As a result, self-exploration and the pursuit of happiness have become integral to the modern notion of love. Relationships are often viewed as spaces for growth, mutual support, and shared experiences, with an emphasis on emotional compatibility and companionship.

Navigating Challenges and Opportunities:

While modernity offers opportunities for greater autonomy and openness, it also presents unique challenges. The fast-paced nature of life, increased work demands, and technological distractions can strain relationships. Balancing the demands of career, personal growth, and emotional connection requires careful navigation and conscious effort.

Redefining Commitment and Longevity:

The modern notion of love challenges traditional notions of commitment and longevity. Relationships are often assessed based on mutual compatibility and emotional well-being, and individuals are encouraged to prioritize their own happiness. Concepts like serial monogamy and open relationships challenge conventional ideals of lifelong partnership.

Cultivating Authentic Connections:

In the midst of the modern complexities surrounding love, there is a yearning for authentic and meaningful connections. Amid the noise of the digital age and the pressures of contemporary life, individuals seek genuine emotional intimacy and a sense of belonging.

In exploring the modern notion of love, we recognize the dynamic interplay between societal changes and individual desires. The impact of technology, globalization, and evolving social structures has redefined how we perceive, pursue, and prioritize love in our lives. By navigating the complexities of the modern landscape, we come to understand that while the external factors may change, the essence of love remains a steadfast and enduring force in the human experience.

Love's Role in Relationships

Love serves as the glue that binds individuals together in a web of relationships—whether romantic, familial, or platonic. It is the intricate dance of emotions, affections, and connections that forms the foundation of our interactions with others. In this chapter, we delve into the multifaceted role of love in different types of relationships, exploring how it contributes to emotional bonding, commitment, and vital support.

Romantic Love:

In romantic relationships, love often takes center stage, driving the passionate yearning and deep emotional connections that characterize such unions. Romantic love fosters intimacy and vulnerability, encouraging individuals to share their innermost thoughts and feelings. It is the force that fuels the desire for companionship, physical affection, and the pursuit of a life partner.

Familial Love:

Familial bonds are often steeped in a unique kind of love—one that is nurtured over years of shared experiences and mutual support. The love between parents and children, siblings, and extended family members provides a safety net of emotional care and understanding. Familial love is characterized by loyalty, acceptance, and the willingness to stand by one another through thick and thin.

Platonic Love and Friendship:

Platonic love, or the affection shared among friends, is equally important in shaping our lives. Friendships offer companionship, shared laughter, and a space for mutual growth. Platonic love is a vital source of emotional support, often providing a safe haven for expressing thoughts and feelings without judgment.

Emotional Bonding and Connection:

Love forms the emotional bedrock of relationships, fostering a sense of connection and understanding between individuals. It enables us to resonate with another person's joys and sorrows, enhancing empathy and compassion. Emotional bonding is the thread that weaves through relationships, allowing us to experience the joys of shared happiness and the solace of shared pain.

Commitment and Shared Goals:

Love is a driving force that underpins commitment in relationships. Whether in romantic partnerships, familial ties, or friendships, love encourages individuals to invest time, effort, and care into nurturing the bond. Commitment involves a willingness to weather challenges, work through conflicts, and support one another's growth.

Navigating Challenges and Providing Support:

Love's role in relationships is particularly evident during times of challenge and adversity. It provides a foundation of emotional support, enabling individuals to lean on one another for strength and encouragement. The unwavering presence of love offers reassurance that, even in difficult moments, someone cares deeply and is willing to stand by your side.

Mutual Growth and Enrichment:

Love in relationships is not static—it evolves and deepens over time. It fosters an environment for mutual growth and enrichment, encouraging individuals to learn from one another, broaden their perspectives, and engage in self-discovery. Love is a catalyst for personal transformation as individuals navigate the intricate paths of their relationships.

In exploring love's role in relationships, we recognize its power to transform and elevate our interactions with others. Whether in the context of romantic partnerships, familial ties, or deep friendships, love weaves a tapestry of emotions, connections, and shared experiences. It is the steadfast force that anchors us in a world of uncertainty, offering the comfort of companionship and the enduring warmth of emotional bonds.

Love and Gender Dynamics

The interplay between love and gender dynamics is a rich and complex tapestry woven from historical legacies, cultural expectations, and evolving societal norms. The ways in which love is understood, expressed, and experienced have been deeply influenced by the roles that society assigns to masculinity and femininity. In this chapter, we delve into the intricate relationship between love and gender dynamics, exploring how historical and psychological factors have shaped these roles and discussing the evolving notions of equality in modern relationships.

Historical Roots of Gender Roles in Love:
   Throughout history, traditional gender roles have often dictated the dynamics of love. Societal expectations have prescribed distinct roles for men and women in relationships, based on notions of strength, protection, and emotional nurturing. These roles influenced how love was expressed, as men and women were often assigned different responsibilities within relationships.

Societal Shifts and Changing Expectations:
   As societies have evolved, so have notions of masculinity and femininity. Social movements, including feminism and gender equality, have challenged traditional gender roles and expectations. The shifting landscape has given rise to a reimagining of what it means to be masculine or feminine within

the context of love and relationships.

Evolving Notions of Masculinity and Femininity:
  The traditional boundaries of masculinity and femininity are being reshaped in the context of love. Men are increasingly encouraged to express vulnerability, empathy, and emotional openness—qualities often associated with femininity. Similarly, women are asserting their independence, ambition, and autonomy, expanding the spectrum of what femininity can encompass.

Equality and Reciprocity in Modern Relationships:
  The pursuit of gender equality has influenced how love is experienced in modern relationships. The concept of partnership has become central, emphasizing shared responsibilities, mutual respect, and a balance of power. Modern couples often strive for reciprocity in emotional support, decision-making, and the division of household and caregiving responsibilities.

Challenges and Intersectionality:
  The evolving landscape of gender dynamics intersects with other aspects of identity, such as race, sexuality, and cultural background. Intersectionality highlights that experiences of love and relationships are shaped not only by gender but also by the unique intersection of various social identities.

Embracing Fluidity and Diversity:
  The modern understanding of love embraces the fluidity of gender roles and encourages individuals to express themselves authentically. Relationships are increasingly seen as spaces where both partners can bring their full selves, transcending traditional expectations and finding a deeper connection based on shared values and mutual understanding.

Striving for Authenticity and Empowerment:
  In the journey towards redefining gender dynamics in love, authenticity and empowerment are key themes. Individuals are encouraged to navigate relationships on their own terms, free from rigid expectations. The goal is

to create partnerships that reflect shared values, emotional intimacy, and mutual growth.

As we explore the interplay between love and gender dynamics, we recognize that societal shifts are reshaping the way love is perceived and experienced. The evolving notions of masculinity, femininity, and equality are transforming relationships into spaces of shared understanding, partnership, and empowerment. By embracing diverse expressions of love and challenging traditional roles, individuals are paving the way for a more inclusive and authentic experience of love in the modern world.

The Science of Lasting Love

The enduring allure of lasting love has captivated scholars, poets, and philosophers for centuries. In the realm of modern psychology, the science of relationships offers insights into the factors that contribute to lasting love and relationship satisfaction. This chapter delves into the scientific foundations of enduring love, exploring the intricate interplay of communication, empathy, shared values, and more, that foster strong and resilient relationships.

Communication: The Bedrock of Connection:
Effective communication lies at the heart of successful relationships. Open and honest conversations allow partners to share thoughts, feelings, and concerns. Active listening, clear expression, and the ability to resolve conflicts constructively promote a deep sense of understanding and emotional connection.

Empathy and Emotional Intimacy:
Empathy—the ability to understand and share the feelings of another—is a cornerstone of lasting love. Partners who can empathize with one another's experiences create a bond built on emotional intimacy. Empathy fosters a safe space for vulnerability and helps partners navigate challenges with compassion and support.

Shared Values and Goals:

Shared values provide a sense of alignment and purpose in a relationship. Partners who have common goals, beliefs, and interests experience a greater sense of unity and camaraderie. These shared foundations create a framework for making decisions, resolving conflicts, and navigating life's journey together.

Friendship and Mutual Respect:
Strong romantic relationships are often rooted in friendship and mutual respect. Treating each other as equals, valuing one another's opinions, and genuinely enjoying each other's company contribute to a sense of camaraderie and companionship. Partners who share a genuine fondness and admiration for each other's character are more likely to weather challenges with resilience.

Quality Time and Rituals:
Spending quality time together and cultivating meaningful rituals can fortify a relationship. Regular interactions, date nights, and shared experiences help partners stay connected and reinforce the bond. Rituals, whether small gestures or significant traditions, provide a sense of stability and nostalgia that contribute to lasting love.

Conflict Resolution and Compromise:
All relationships encounter conflicts, but how they are resolved matters deeply. Partners who can address disagreements with respect, empathy, and a willingness to compromise foster an environment of understanding and growth. Conflict resolution skills enhance emotional connection and prevent resentment from taking root.

Emotional Support and Intimacy:
Emotional support forms the backbone of lasting love. Partners who feel understood, valued, and validated by each other create a foundation of trust and security. Intimacy—both emotional and physical—fosters a sense of closeness and belonging, creating a space where vulnerability can thrive.

Continuous Growth and Adaptation:

Lasting love is a journey of growth and adaptation. Partners who encourage each other's personal development and navigate life's changes together create a sense of partnership that endures through time. Flexibility, willingness to learn, and a shared commitment to growth contribute to relationship longevity.

The Science of Lasting Love: A Dynamic Process:

The science of lasting love reveals that relationships are dynamic processes shaped by ongoing efforts, intentional actions, and a deep understanding of one another. By cultivating effective communication, empathy, shared values, and other key factors, individuals can foster relationships that not only withstand the test of time but also thrive in the face of challenges.

As we delve into the scientific underpinnings of lasting love, we recognize that the art of maintaining a strong and fulfilling relationship is grounded in knowledge, intention, and the willingness to continually invest in one another's well-being. Through understanding the factors that contribute to relationship satisfaction, individuals can navigate the intricate landscape of love with greater insight and purpose.

Reflection and Future Perspectives

As we draw our journey through the intricate terrain of love to a close, it's time to reflect on the profound insights gained from historical exploration and psychological inquiry. This chapter offers a panoramic view of the evolution of love from multiple perspectives and synthesizes the key takeaways that illuminate the essence of this complex emotion. Additionally, we consider the potential future shifts in understanding love, offering a glimpse into the paths that this timeless concept may traverse in the ever-changing landscape of human experience.

Reflecting on the Historical Tapestry of Love:

From ancient civilizations to the modern world, the historical tapestry of love reveals the enduring significance of this emotion in human lives. We have witnessed how love has been influenced by societal norms, cultural values, and the ebb and flow of human interactions. The evolution of love showcases its resilience, adaptability, and transformative power across centuries and civilizations.

Synthesizing Psychological Insights:

The exploration of love from psychological viewpoints has illuminated the intricate mechanisms that underlie our emotional connections. From attachment styles to cognitive processes, psychological theories have offered frameworks to understand the dynamics of love in relationships. Empathy, communication, and shared values emerged as pivotal factors that nurture strong and lasting bonds.

Key Takeaways on the Essence of Love:
Through our journey, we've gleaned several key takeaways that underscore the essence of love:
- Love is a multifaceted and dynamic emotion that transcends time and culture.
- It is shaped by historical narratives, psychological processes, and evolving societal norms.
- Love involves emotional bonds, mutual respect, and shared experiences.
- Effective communication, empathy, and shared values are cornerstones of lasting love.
- Gender dynamics are evolving, reshaping how love is understood and experienced.
- Love is a force that thrives on authenticity, growth, and adaptation.

Future Shifts in Understanding Love:
As society continues to evolve, the understanding of love is likely to undergo further transformation. Here are some potential future shifts to consider:
- Technological advancements may reshape how love is experienced, challenging notions of intimacy and connection.
- The ongoing pursuit of gender equality may lead to more equitable and balanced partnerships.
- Cultural diversity and globalization may enrich our understanding of love by exposing us to varied perspectives and practices.
- Psychological research may uncover deeper layers of emotional intricacies within relationships, leading to more nuanced insights.

A Call to Embrace Love's Complexity:
As we reflect on the evolution of love, we recognize its complexity, its ability to adapt, and its capacity to withstand the test of time. In an ever-changing world, love remains a constant thread that binds humanity together. It invites

us to explore our own hearts, forge meaningful connections, and embrace the diverse forms of love that enrich our lives.

Embracing the Journey Ahead:

As we conclude our exploration of the evolution of love, we embark on a future where love's landscape continues to shift, adapt, and flourish. We carry with us the wisdom of history, the insights of psychology, and the warmth of authentic connections. Let us navigate this journey with open hearts, embracing the unending potential of love to shape, transform, and inspire our lives in ways we have yet to imagine.

www.ingramcontent.com/pod-product-compliance
Lightning Source LLC
LaVergne TN
LVHW020458080526
838202LV00057B/6033